T0128614

SONGS THROUGH TRIALS

HARMONY

WestBow Press books may be ordered through booksellers or by contacting:

WestBow Press
A Division of Thomas Nelson & Zondervan
1663 Liberty Drive
Bloomington, IN 47403
www.westbowpress.com
1 (866) 928-1240

Because of the dynamic nature of the Internet, any web addresses or links contained in this book may have changed since publication and may no longer be valid. The views expressed in this work are solely those of the author and do not necessarily reflect the views of the publisher, and the publisher hereby disclaims any responsibility for them.

Any people depicted in stock imagery provided by Getty Images are models, and such images are being used for illustrative purposes only.
Certain stock imagery © Getty Images.

Scripture quotations marked (NIV) are taken from the Holy Bible, New International Version®, NIV®. Copyright © 1973, 1978, 1984, 2011 by Biblica, Inc.® Used by permission of Zondervan. All rights reserved worldwide. www.zondervan.com The "NIV" and "New International Version" are trademarks registered in the United States Patent and Trademark Office by Biblica, Inc.®

Scripture marked (KJV) taken from the King James Version of the Bible.

Scripture marked (NKJV) taken from the New King James Version®. Copyright © 1982 by Thomas Nelson. Used by permission. All rights reserved.

ISBN: 978-1-9736-9612-4 (sc)
ISBN: 978-1-9736-9613-1 (e)

Library of Congress Control Number: 2020911941

Print information available on the last page.

WestBow Press rev. date: 09/02/2020

WESTBOW
PRESS®
A DIVISION OF THOMAS NELSON
& ZONDERVAN

SONGS THROUGH TRIALS

Nothing Can Shake You

Nothing can shake you
When you're in The Shadow
The Shadow of Almighty God
When all of the trials
Are multiplying
When we're all
Crying~

We trust and rest In His Arms! We trust and rest In His Arms! We trust~
We rest in His Arms!

The terror around us
Will not confound us
We stand firm
In His Love
If His saving grace
You've freely taken
You will never be forsaken!
We trust- we rest in His Love! We trust and rest in His Love! We trust- we rest in
His Love!

Whoever dwells in the shelter of

The Most High

will Rest in the Shadow of

The Almighty.

Psalm 91:1NIV

Concerns or Worries	Prayer or Bible Verse

I Confess

I confess my unfaithfulness
To The Only One Who is faithful
I confess my unwillingness
To completely follow at times

He says
Come to Me
Why do we run away?
He says
Follow Me
Why do we go astray?

He says confess
I will forgive
He'll heal this land
And help us to live
To give honor in all we do
Lord, Let Your Spirit shine right through
He says
Come to Me
Why do we run away?
He says follow Me
Why do we go astray? (Repeat)

Lord we come to You
We confess our sin
Please cleanse us
And heal us from within

Lord, we
seek Your Face
And Praise You
For Your Grace
Lord, we run to You
Let Your Love Shine Through!

I confess my unfaithfulness
To The Only One Who is Faithful
I commit now to follow You
Lord, Let Your Spirit shine right through!

If we *confess* our sins, He is *faithful* and just to forgive us our sins and to cleanse us from all unrighteousness.

1 John 1:9 KJV

Matthew 11:28-30 NIV
"Come to me,
    all you who are weary and
burdened,
        and I will give you
rest.

Take my yoke
upon you
and learn from me,

for I am *gentle* and humble in heart,

and you will find
Rest *for your souls.*

Thank you, God that you forgive me and for how you will work in each situation:

_____
_____
_____
_____
_____
_____
_____
_____
_____
_____
_____
_____
_____
_____
_____
_____
_____
_____
_____
_____
_____
_____
_____

I pray out of His glorious riches He may strengthen you with power through His Spirit in your inner being, so that Christ may dwell in your hearts through faith.

I pray that you, being rooted and established in love, may have power together with all The Lord's holy people, to grasp how wide and long and high and deep is the Love of Christ, and to know this Love that surpasses knowledge-that you may be filled to the measure of all the fullness of God. *Ephesians 3:16-19 NIV*

"Our Lives Are Like a Song"

Our lives are like a song
Are we out of tune?
Do we exude Hope
We will see God soon?

(Chorus)
May my whole life from now on
Be a beautiful song
Lord, let Your grace shine upon
May others join along
In a beautiful song
Help us glorify You
In all we say and do
Please stop our sin before it starts
Cleanse and heal our hearts

Our lives are like a song
Help us sing in unity
May the melody You see
Bring You Glory (Sing Chorus)

Our lives are like a song
Do we share the Joy inside?
Overflowing Faith and Love
Will be displayed if we abide
(Sing Chorus)

¹ I waited patiently for the LORD;

He turned to me and heard my cry.

² He lifted me out of the slimy pit,
out of the mud and mire;
He set my feet on a rock
and gave me a firm place to stand.

He put a new song in my mouth,

a hymn of praise to our God.

Many will see and
fear the LORD
and

put their trust
in The LORD.
Psalm 40:1-3NIV

Write a new song:)

"Stir Our Hearts"

Choir Song

Break our hearts once again
(Once again)
To show Love and Compassion
(Love and Compassion)
We have wandered away
(So far away)
Bring us back today
(Please bring us back today)

Let Your Love overflow
(Overflow)
So others will know
(Help them to know)
Your Amazing Love is True
(So True)
Help us trust in You
(Lord we trust in You)
We believe you died to pay the price
(You paid our price)
The Blameless Sacrifice
(Perfect Sacrifice)
We trust and ask You to forgive

(Please forgive)
All of our sin
(Please heal us from within)

Stir our hearts once again
(Once again)
It's time to take a stand
(Time to take a stand)
Cleanse our hearts from sin
(From sin)
Please heal this land
(Heal this land)
Stir our hearts once again
(Once again)
To Love and follow You
(Help us follow You)

Cleanse our hearts once again
(Once again)
Please heal this land
(Heal this land)
Stir our hearts once again
(Once again)
It's time to Love again!

How God has renewed me today:

How can I share God's Love today?

Lord, I am praising You during this time of life.

"Song of Deliverance"
(A song for a soul-singing choir)

Nailed to the cross
Arms opened wide
Nothing but Love
Overflowing Love inside
Nailed to the cross
Arms open wide
Nothing but Love - He laid down His Life
He's still waiting for you
To let Him come inside
His Arms are still open wide-

HE will deliver
He will deliver you
He will deliver
God will deliver you(Repeat)
Break free from sin
Abide with Him
Break free from sin
Abide with Him

He'll give you songs of deliverance
With each step of obedience
Praise songs that will make you dance
Sweet songs of deliverance
Oh, He was
Nailed to the cross
Arms opened wide
Nothing but Love
Overflowing Love inside
Nailed to the cross to
Pay our price
Overflowing Love
Jesus, our perfect sacrifice
Nailed to the cross
To set us free from sin
Believe on Him- he says
He will forgive, He will deliver
He will deliver you
He will deliver
God will give you songs of deliverance!

⁷You are my hiding place;

You will protect me from trouble

and surround me with

Songs of Deliverance.

Psalm 32:7 NIV

Please write some ways God has worked all things together for your good~

If My people,

who are called by My name,

will humble themselves, and Pray, and seek My face, and turn from their wicked ways, then I will

hear from heaven,
and will
Forgive
their sin, and
Heal their land.
2 Chronicles 7:14 NKJV

Favorite Bible Verses:

From the rising of the sun to the place where it sets, the name of the LORD is to be praised. *Psalm 113:3 NIV*

About the Author

The goal she has through sharing these songs/ poems is to encourage, comfort and inspire others through storms and trials in life.

Printed in the United States
By Bookmasters